CHRISTOPHER TAYLOR

THE ARCHAEOLOGY
OF GARDENS

SHIRE ARCHAEOLOGY

2

Cover photograph
Garden remains, including two gateways, at Holdenby, Northamptonshire.

For Collins Bowen, who taught me.

Published by
SHIRE PUBLICATIONS LTD
Cromwell House, Church Street, Princes Risborough,
Aylesbury, Bucks, HP17 9AJ, UK.

Series Editor: James Dyer

ISBN 0 85263 625 3

First published 1983

Set in 11 point Times and printed in Great Britain by C. I. Thomas & Sons
(Haverfordwest) Ltd, Press Buildings, Merlins Bridge, Haverfordwest.

Contents

Acknowledgements

My greatest debt is to the Royal Commission on Historical Monuments (England) as it was the Commission that gave me the opportunity to discover abandoned gardens. I am especially grateful to the Commissioners, through their Secretary, Dr P. J. Fowler, for giving me permission to reproduce a number of plans and photographs of sites described in the Inventories of the Commission. I would also like to thank Mr D. R. Wilson for assistance with the aerial photographs and Mr B. Thomason for undertaking the preparation of the figures. My special thanks go to Mrs M. Hegerty, not only for the work carried out on the manuscript but also for similar help over many years.

4

List of Illustrations

1
Introduction

What is a garden? In essence there are two basic types, although there is not always a clear division between them in practice. The first, and arguably the most interesting, is what may be termed the 'pleasure garden'. It is this which is our primary concern. A pleasure garden may be defined as a relatively small area of land in which a variety of plants, trees and shrubs are deliberately arranged and managed to create contrived patterns of shape and colour. The main purpose of this garden is, in the first instance, to give satisfaction to its owner or creator, though it may also be a deliberate attempt to indicate status or social achievement. Such a garden is a visual expression of the aims, desires or attitudes of that person in the setting of contemporary society. A pleasure garden is therefore an art form of a rather special kind.

The second type may be called the 'vegetable garden'. This is often an equally small piece of land on which different varieties of plants and trees are grown in order to produce food by intensive agricultural methods, usually for the owner's own consumption. It thus has a mainly utilitarian purpose. Both types of garden are attempts to order the natural world to provide their creators with aesthetic or material satisfaction.

What is archaeology? It is the scientific study of the past by the examination of the material remains left behind by previous generations. Though many people equate archaeology with excavation, the understanding of the past by archaeology involves much more than merely digging. When an archaeological site exists as an upstanding series of mounds, banks or ditches these features can be planned and interpreted by analytical fieldwork. Where sites have been obliterated by later activities they can be discovered and interpreted by using air photographs, by geophysical methods using sophisticated sensing devices and by the minute examination of the ground for traces of objects which have been exposed by modern disturbance.

The archaeology of gardens is thus the examination of the sites of abandoned gardens by all the methods outlined above. Using them, the remains of abandoned gardens can be identified, recorded, examined and understood in the same way as a bronze age burial mound or a deserted medieval village.

It may seem, at first sight, difficult to study by such

archaeological methods features which are basically transitory arrangements of plants. Yet this is not so. For the very ordering of plants into a desired pattern, whether for pleasure or for food, involves disturbance of the ground and the use of material objects. The construction of boundary walls or fences, ponds, flower beds, paths and terraces leaves traces in various forms which the archaeologist can study. The raised terrace of a seventeenth-century garden is a constructed earthwork which can be examined and interpreted in the same way as the rampart of an iron age hillfort. Similarly the edging of a Roman flower bed can leave the same kind of feature hidden beneath the ground as that which marks the circumference of a bronze age hut and thus can be revealed and understood by identical archaeological methods. There is thus no reason why archaeologists should not study gardens and, by using their techniques, help towards the understanding of an important and interesting aspect of the history of man and his environment.

Despite this, however, the archaeology of gardens is a relatively new subject which has not been developed to its full potential. Most archaeologists have, perhaps inevitably, been concerned to understand the settlements, burial places and religious sites of past periods and, even when they work on those aspects which involve the cultivation of land, there has been a tendency to study somewhat wider canvases such as fields or field systems. Because the existence of gardens has not been appreciated they have not been looked for and thus not found.

It is probable that most Roman villas in Britain had pleasure gardens of some form. Yet with a few notable exceptions archaeologists, when excavating villas, have been more concerned with the economic activities of such places. Courtyards have been examined, pathways discovered, small timber structures found, but all have usually been interpreted as features which were connected with farming practices. The paths are said to lead to stables, the timber structures to be pig pens or sheep folds. Few archaeologists have considered that the paths may have divided flower beds or that the structures could be the foundations of summerhouses or pergolas. In other cases the archaeologists have concentrated their work on the main building of the villa and have not attempted to discover any features which would suggest adjacent gardens.

For example, at the villa at Apethorpe in Northamptonshire, excavations in 1859 led to the discovery of a typical Roman villa with buildings arranged around a central courtyard (fig. 1). In the

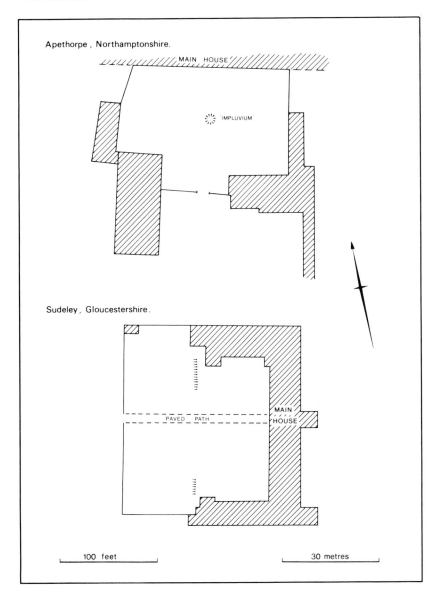

Fig. 1. Archaeological evidence of gardens at two Roman villas. (After RCHM.)

exact centre of this courtyard a shallow stone-lined depression
was found which was described by the excavator as an 'implu-
vium'. This was later re-interpreted as a 'dipping well' but it
seems much more likely to have been a central water feature in a
garden. Similarly the long narrow structures on two sides of the
central courtyard of a Roman villa at Pitney, in Somerset, have
been interpreted as pigsties and slaves' quarters. The position of
these, adjacent to and facing on to the splendid facade of the
imposing villa, makes this unlikely, but the possibility that they
were garden pavilions of some kind has never been entertained.

The same lack of appreciation of the existence of gardens has
led to confusion on sites of later date. The complex earthworks
which surround the almost isolated church at Steeple Gidding, in
Cambridgeshire, have in the past been confidently interpreted as
the remains of the deserted village of Steeple Gidding, whose
well documented existence came to an end in the mid fourteenth
century (fig. 2). Yet while a large proportion of these earthworks
do indeed represent the streets, houses and closes of the former
village, the raised terraces and the system of rectangular ponds
are the remains of a garden laid out on top of the long abandoned
village in 1648 around a house then newly built. At Old Warden,
in Bedfordshire, the extensive earthwork remains of the great
Cistercian abbey, swept away in the middle of the sixteenth
century, are partly overlain by the terraces of a late sixteenth-
century garden.

None of these gardens was recognised until recently because,
as is so often the case, archaeologists only see what they want to
see. If they have been told that a site is a deserted village then the
visible remains are interpreted as part of one. The three-sided
moat in the centre of the deserted village of Papley, Northamptonshire, was for long assumed to be the site of the medieval
manor house. Yet close examination, combined with some simple
historical research, proved that it is the boundary ditch of an early
seventeenth-century garden associated with the house which was
built there fifty years after the village had disappeared and which
was demolished in the 1670s (plate 1). The same is true at
Newton, also in Northamptonshire (plate 2). The now isolated
church and the adjacent banks and scarps all indicate the site of a
lost village. The village did indeed exist, and at this place. But the
earthworks are the remains of an elaborate garden built by the
Tresham family in the late sixteenth century for a new house
there. Both house and garden were abandoned in the early
eighteenth century.

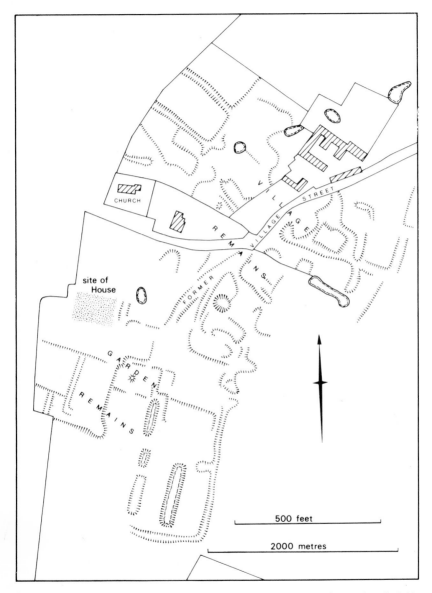

Fig. 2. Steeple Gidding, Cambridgeshire. Most of the earthworks at the north end of this site are the remains of the village of Steeple Gidding which was finally abandoned in the fourteenth century. To the south, the more regular pattern of scarps, banks and ponds consists of fragments of the mid seventeenth-century gardens.

Plate 1. Deserted village of Papley, Northamptonshire. The U-shaped ditch, edged with trees, is part of a late sixteenth- or early seventeenth-century garden, associated with a contemporary house which stood near the pond. The surrounding earthworks are the remains of the medieval village of Papley, finally depopulated for sheep in the mid sixteenth century. (Copyright: Cambridge University Collection.)

Plate 2. Deserted village of Newton, Northamptonshire. The isolated church indicates that there was once a village here, but the earthworks in the lower foreground, partly destroyed by an old ironstone quarry, are those of a formal garden and house of the late sixteenth century. (Copyright: Cambridge University Collection.)

Plate 3. Site of garden, Woodford, Northamptonshire. These terraces, overlooking the river Nene, are part of an early seventeenth-century garden. (Crown Copyright.)

At Woodford, Northamptonshire, a massive series of terraces, bounded by high banks, is traditionally said to be the site of one of Cromwell's gun batteries, though what it was to protect is not clear (plate 3). In fact the site is that of a house and garden built in 1621 by the St John family and left derelict probably in the late eighteenth or nineteenth century.

There are probably many hundreds of abandoned medieval and post-medieval gardens whose terraces, ponds and flower beds still exist as earthworks, preserved in pasture or hidden in woods, which have never been recognised and remain to be discovered. Indeed, the sites of abandoned pleasure gardens constitute one of the most common types of all upstanding archaeological remains in Britain. There is thus considerable scope for archaeologists, using all the techniques available to them, to examine gardens.

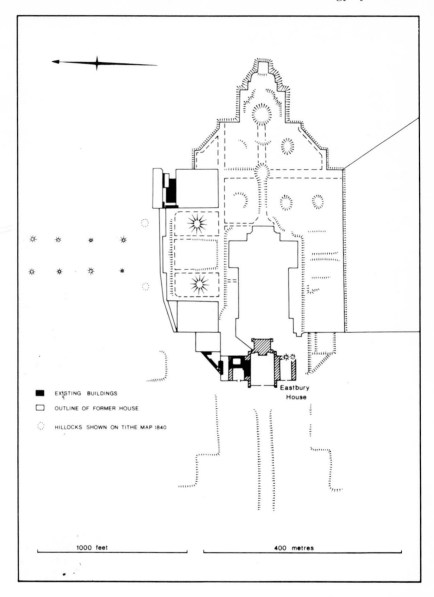

EXISTING BUILDINGS

OUTLINE OF FORMER HOUSE

HILLOCKS SHOWN ON TITHE MAP 1840

Eastbury
House

1000 feet

400 metres

Fig. 3. Eastbury, Dorset. The great house here was largely demolished in 1775, but the complex gardens, as well as part of the surrounding park layout, all dating from the early eighteenth century, have been preserved in pasture and woodland. (After RCHM.)

2
The survival of gardens

Perhaps the first question that may be asked concerning abandoned gardens is why they survive at all? The short answer is that almost all aspects of man's activity survive in some form or another and that, as the construction and management of gardens is one such activity, inevitably some will remain to be studied by archaeologists. We have already noted that the creation of any form of garden involves the disturbance of the soil so that, given that thousands of gardens of all types have been created over the past four thousand years, a certain proportion of them will have survived in some way.

More puzzling perhaps is why very large and elaborate gardens of the late medieval and post-medieval period should have been abandoned, especially the very complex pleasure gardens of the sixteenth and seventeenth centuries. Probably the great majority of these gardens have been completely destroyed. The concept of an ideal pleasure garden has changed radically many times in the past four hundred years. Gardens, like the houses they surrounded, reacted to changing fashions and attitudes. Just as a late sixteenth-century house was very different from a late eighteenth-century one, so the contemporary gardens of these buildings were totally different. Where there has been a house on the same site since the early seventeenth century the present garden will bear little or no relationship to the original one and will be a result of many and considerable changes over the centuries as the aspirations, status and wealth of its owners changed and fashions in garden design altered. Such gardens have little to offer the archaeologist. The splendid nineteenth-century recreation of clipped box hedges in a sixteenth-century style at Longleat House in Wiltshire and the magnificent twentieth-century reconstruction of a late seventeenth-century French garden at Oxburgh Hall, Norfolk, are a delight to the eye as well as being of considerable interest in the understanding of details of plants, colours and layouts. But this is not garden archaeology. The archaeologist has to examine the sites of abandoned gardens if he is to understand their detailed development.

Abandoned pleasure gardens dating from the fourteenth century onwards survive in various forms as a result of many factors, but amongst them are four which are the most important.

Plate 4. House and garden remains, Gamlingay, Cambridgeshire. The former house, built in 1712, lay in the centre of the picture. The uneven rectangular depression marks its cellar. To the left is a circular sunken garden; to the right are terraces and gardens sloping down to a former lake. A line of contemporary ponds lies in the bottom right while top left are traces of walled compartments and flower beds (see also fig. 4). (Copyright: Cambridge University Collection.)

The first, and certainly the most common, is the situation where a large house was built, or perhaps rebuilt, a contemporary garden laid out around it and then the house deserted, often within a relatively short time, before any alterations to either it or its gardens were carried out. Though at first sight this would seem to be an unusual occurrence, it has taken place many times.

Thus at Eastbury, in Dorset, the great house was built between 1717 and 1738 for the wildly eccentric George Bubb Doddington and the gardens were laid out by Charles Bridgeman at the same time (fig. 3). On Doddington's death in 1762 the house was unwanted and was almost completely demolished about 1775. The land occupied by the formal gardens was then incorporated into the landscaped park of the nearby Gunville House, erected about 1795, and all the former flower beds, terraces, ponds and mounts were fortuitously preserved in pasture and within new copses. Similarly at Gamlingay, in Cambridgeshire, a house and its extraordinarily elaborate gardens were constructed in 1712 for Sir George Downing the Third and then abandoned in 1776 and the area returned to grassland. Again the house foundations, garden wall footings, ponds and terraces still survive in the pasture (plate 4; fig. 4).

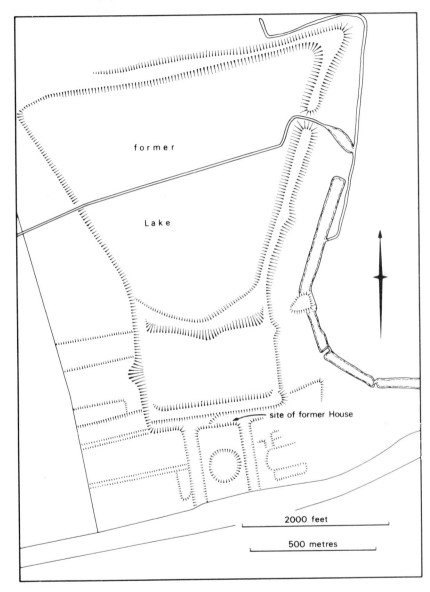

Fig. 4. Gamlingay, Cambridgeshire. These gardens, ponds and lake were all laid out in 1712 for Sir George Downing. They lasted less than sixty years and were then abandoned (see also plate 4). (After RCHM.)

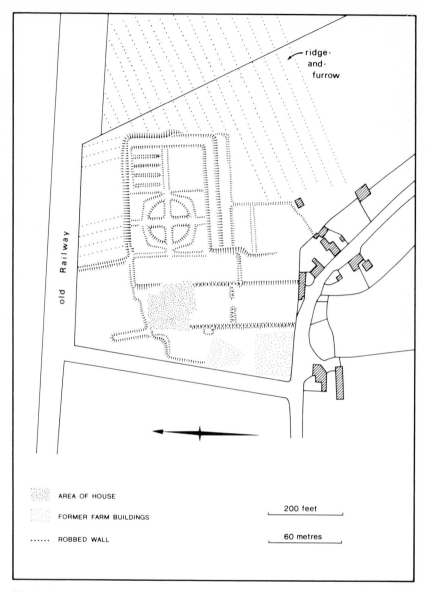

ridge·
and·
furrow

old Railway

AREA OF HOUSE

FORMER FARM BUILDINGS

······ ROBBED WALL

200 feet

60 metres

Fig. 5. Wakerley, Northamptonshire. The gardens here date from 1613, when they were laid out across land which was part of the medieval fields of Wakerley. A detailed survey of the site enabled the arrangements of the original flower beds to be recovered (see also plate 5). (After RCHM.)

Plate 5. House and garden remains, Wakerley, Northamptonshire. The irregular mounds right of centre are the foundations of a house erected soon after 1613. To the left, bounded by terraces, is a broad area in which the original flower beds can be seen. Beyond the house are the footings of walls bounding rectangular compartments (see also fig. 5). (Copyright: Cambridge University Collection.)

At Wakerley, in Northamptonshire, a new house was built soon after 1613 for Sir Richard Cecil, second son of the first Earl of Exeter, and a remarkable garden laid out around it. The house was demolished in 1633 on Cecil's death and again the land was returned to pasture. This grassland has once more preserved all the details including the arrangement of the flower beds (plates 5, 6; fig. 5).

Another factor which has led to the survival of gardens is the change from formal gardens to landscaped parks in the mid eighteenth century. Earlier gardens were often grassed over and left untouched in the new parkland. This relatively sudden change in fashion for the ideal setting of a great house resulted in the fossilisation of many earlier gardens. Those at Boughton, in Northamptonshire, laid out between 1683 and 1740, suffered this fate soon after 1750 when the area was converted to parkland (plates 7, 8). At Cottesbrooke, in the same county, the landscaped park of about 1770 preserved, largely intact, the formal terraced garden laid out between 1702 and 1712 to the north-west of the contemporary house (fig. 6).

The third situation which allows former gardens to survive is

Plate 6. House and garden remains, Wakerley, Northamptonshire. The site of the house is in the foreground. Beyond lie the terraces bounding the main part of the garden (see also fig. 5). (Crown Copyright.)

that where either the intended house or the gardens, or both, were never completed. The unique garden remains at Lyveden New Bield, Northamptonshire, were begun by Sir Thomas Tresham soon after 1597 but they were still incomplete when Tresham died in 1605 and the whole site was abandoned (fig. 7).

Finally the preservation of a garden may be brought about by the declining status of a former great house which results in a contraction of the original area or its partial fossilisation. Haslingfield Hall, Cambridgeshire, is an example of fossilisation. The house was built about 1555 by Thomas Wendy, physician to Henry VIII, but it was remodelled and a moated garden added, probably in the 1660s by Sir Thomas Wendy. Sir Thomas died in 1673 and, though his widow lived on for twenty-three years, the house fell into decay and by 1714 was ruinous and empty. The bulk of the building was later demolished and, though what remained was subsequently repaired and reoccupied, its status as a farmhouse led to the preservation of the original garden, which includes a three-sided moat crossed by a delightful brick bridge (plate 9).

The contraction of a garden as a result of a similar decline in status can be seen at Fen Ditton, Cambridgeshire. The hall there

Plate 7. Garden remains, Boughton, Northamptonshire. The rectangular lake in the foreground replaced an earlier octagonal one in 1721. The trees in the background stand on terraces which once provided walkways from which lower land sloping up to the house was viewed. This area was originally occupied by flower beds and small ponds (see also fig. 11). (Crown Copyright.)

Plate 8. Garden remains, Boughton, Northamptonshire. The trees on the terraces were planted in the eighteenth century when the formal gardens occupying this area were grassed over and made part of the great park (see also fig. 11). (Crown Copyright.)

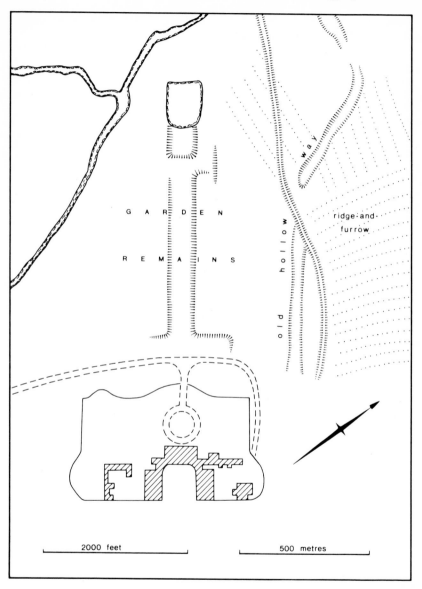

Fig. 6. Cottesbrooke, Northamptonshire. The hall was built between 1702 and 1712 and formal gardens were laid out to the north-west of it. These survived until 1770 when the area was landscaped into a park. This park has preserved some fragments of the earlier garden. (After RCHM.)

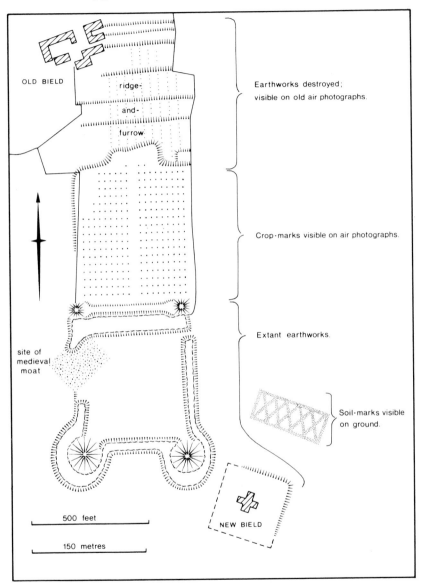

OLD BIELD

ridge-
and-
furrow

site of
medieval
moat

500 feet

150 metres

NEW BIELD

Earthworks destroyed;
visible on old air photographs.

Crop-marks visible on air photographs.

Extant earthworks.

Soil-marks visible
on ground.

Fig. 7. Lyveden, Northamptonshire. These unfinished gardens of 1597 were intended to lie near a house, on the site of the Old Bield, which was never constructed. They illustrate not only yet another variant of elaborate sixteenth-century gardens, but also the various means by which archaeologists can recover the evidence of such gardens.

Plate 9. A seventeenth-century bridge, Haslingfield Hall, Cambridgeshire. The bridge was constructed to carry the main drive to the house over a contemporary moat, dug to enclose the formal garden there. (Crown Copyright.)

was largely rebuilt in the 1630s and formal gardens were added in the late seventeenth or early eighteenth century. But again the house declined in status and passed quickly through the hands of a variety of owners. One of these, before 1807, reduced the size of the garden, remodelled what remained and so left some of the original ponds and terraces preserved in an adjacent paddock.

Sometimes it is not clear why or even when a great house and its garden disappeared. The magnificent gardens at Harrington, Northamptonshire, probably date from about 1680. They were arranged in broad terraces laid out across sloping ground and the traces of ponds, walkways and even flower beds still survive, as does the site of the original house at the lower end (plates 10, 11, 12). Yet while it certainly existed in 1712, its subsequent history is quite unknown.

The same is true of the gardens at Alderton, Northamptonshire (plate 13). These were laid out by William Gorges in 1582 when a large mansion was built there. The house seems to have been demolished before 1726, though when is not certain. Now only the terraces, ponds and a huge motte-like prospect mound remain, surrounded by medieval plough ridges and the abandoned lanes, paddocks and house sites of what was once a much larger village of Alderton.

Plate 10. House and garden remains, Harrington, Northamptonshire. These remarkable gardens consist of a series of broad terraces extending down the hillside. The upper three terraces have ponds of various shapes cut into them, while traces of footpaths and flower beds may be seen on the two lower terraces. The two grooves crossing the terraces and meeting at the top are a contemporary circular walk. Slightly right of centre an area of uneven ground marks the site of the house with, beyond, a sunken garden edged by further terraces and occupied by a central pond and footpath. (Copyright: Cambridge University Collection.)

Plate 11. Garden remains, Harrington, Northamptonshire. A view of the large pond on the central terrace. This pond and the others are on limestone and were therefore lined with puddled clay, which has been exposed by cattle-treading in places. (Crown Copyright.)

Plate 12. Garden remains, Harrington, Northamptonshire. A view of the upper terraces. In the foreground is the approach drive to the house. The depressions are the sites of trees which were planted alongside this drive. (Crown Copyright.)

Plate 13. Garden remains, Alderton, Northamptonshire. In the centre of the picture stands a huge circular mound, originally a prospect mound overlooking the terraced gardens to the right. Below is a series of contemporary ponds. The original house, built in 1582, at the same time as the gardens were created, probably stood below the terraces and to the left of the road, on the ground occupied by the farm buildings and stockyards. Other earthworks in the photograph are the abandoned lanes, house sites and paddocks of medieval Alderton. (Copyright: Cambridge University Collection.)

3
Prehistoric and Roman gardens

Now we have established that abandoned gardens can exist, the next question is what should archaeologists look for when attempting to discover and understand them? The answer depends on their date, whether Roman, medieval or later, and their condition, whether they survive as earthworks or are buried below ground.

Perhaps the best way to answer the question is to examine the archaeological evidence for gardens at different periods and thus see what might be found elsewhere. At present there is no evidence for pleasure gardens in Britain before the Roman period. This is not to say that they did not exist, for prehistoric society was primitive only in its technology. In every other aspect it was as complex and as sophisticated as our own. Despite living, allegedly, at or near subsistence levels, most prehistoric cultures in Britain found the time and resources to indulge in numerous activities which, at least to our eyes, were not directly connected with food production. The evidence of the thousands of elaborate burial mounds of neolithic and bronze age date showed that people expended considerable resources in ritual and ceremony. Throughout the whole of prehistoric time the occurrence of precious objects, of undoubted aesthetic merit by any standards, shows that creative expression in all its forms was appreciated, sought after and supplied by highly skilled artists and craftsmen. There is thus no reason to suppose that prehistoric people could not have had pleasure gardens of some form even if, as yet, our archaeological techniques have not discovered them.

Certainly there were vegetable gardens in prehistoric times but even these are little known or understood and cannot be readily distinguished from small paddocks used for other agricultural purposes. The earliest vegetable gardens must have appeared around 5000 BC, in the early neolithic period, when man first learnt to cultivate plots for food. As far as we can see, cultivation of small plots by the use of digging sticks or stone hoes predated the arrival of the plough and thus of agriculture in its widest sense. The small, perhaps temporary, plots of the earliest nomadic neolithic groups may be considered as the first gardens of Britain. Later on, and certainly by the middle of the neolithic period, around 3000 BC, settlement became more permanent, and properly protected and fenced plots or gardens became characteristic features of the majority of occupied areas. From then until the end of the prehistoric period there is evidence for such gardens.

There are problems of definition here. Should small enclosed areas of land, adjacent to houses, be called gardens or could they be termed small fields? And were such plots always used for growing plants or did they have other functions, notably as animal paddocks or farmyards? The problem of distinguishing garden plots from small fields is almost impossible to solve. Theoretically fields are ploughed, gardens are not, and in addition fields are normally said to be given over to one main crop at any one time, while gardens have various crops. By the very nature of archaeological evidence it is often impossible to ascertain all or indeed any of these features. An even greater problem, as noted earlier, is that archaeologists have been lacking in enthusiasm for gardens. In a lengthy collection of papers from a conference on prehistoric land allotment there is no reference to vegetable gardens of either prehistoric or Roman date. Every contributor was entirely concerned with fields.

As archaeological methods have become more sophisticated it is possible to recover evidence of plough marks cut into the subsoil or underlying rocks and so distinguish true fields from garden plots. It is also becoming possible to distinguish, in some cases, enclosures which may have been primarily for stock as opposed to cultivation. Palaeobotanical research can now identify the crops grown in fields and plots alike by means of techniques such as pollen analysis and seed identification, though this still cannot distinguish between fields and plots. In the main, however, we have to rely on less convincing ways of identifying gardens of the prehistoric period, that of physical shape and size as revealed by ground examination, air photography or excavation. In those parts of Britain, mainly the upland areas or on marginal land, where prehistoric settlements and fields are untouched by later activities, it is possible to examine on the ground the remains of presumed prehistoric gardens even though, until excavation takes place, there can be no certainty in their identification. For example at Ewe Close, Crosby Ravensworth, in Cumbria, the stone-built huts, paddocks and closes of a small settlement lie on the open moorland (plate 14). It has never been excavated and may be of either iron age or Roman date. While the larger paddocks are likely to have been for the penning of animals, the small plots which are actually attached to the huts

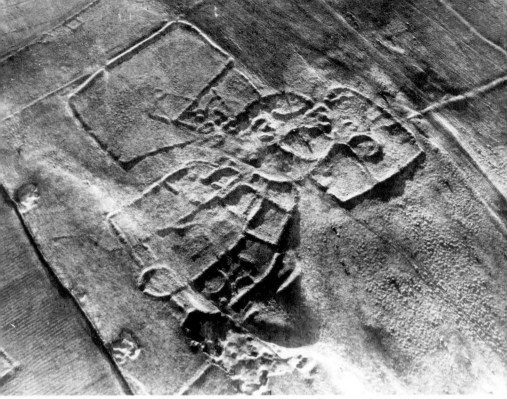

Plate 14. Iron age or native Roman settlement, Crosby Ravensworth, Cumbria. The circular stone houses and walled enclosures are the remains of a small hamlet. The larger enclosures are certainly paddocks or stockyards, but the smaller ones attached to the house sites may have been used as garden plots. (Copyright: Cambridge University Collection.)

may have been used, at least in part, as gardens, producing special crops for domestic consumption.

Such extant remains of possible gardens and indeed the associated fields and settlements are increasingly rare as modern agricultural activities destroy more and more of them. Elsewhere the only way of identifying the complex patterns of prehistoric occupation is by the use of air photography. Under suitable conditions of soil and modern crops the traces of ditches, banks, pits and other disturbances of the ground are revealed from the air. As a result of intensive aerial reconnaissance many thousands of prehistoric settlement sites are now known to have existed in almost every part of Britain. Many of these have features which may well be the traces of garden plots, associated with houses.

An instance of this may be seen at a site at Thorpe Achurch, Northamptonshire. Detailed examination of the ground has revealed iron age pottery and thus the pattern of crop marks visible from the air probably represents the site of an iron age village (plate 15). It consists of a series of enclosures lying on either side of a ditched trackway running north to south. Within some of the enclosures or closes are traces of circular huts and in others large pits, probably used for grain storage. On the other hand a few plots have no features within them. Only excavation could finally prove their purpose and certainly they may well be stockyards. On the other hand they could equally well be garden plots.

Excavation is usually considered to be the final arbiter in problems of archaeological sites. However, with prehistoric gardens this may not be easy, partly because of the difficulty in finding, even by excavation, incontrovertible evidence that an area of land was used as a vegetable garden. Few gardens have been identified with certainty. At a neolithic and bronze age site near Hurst Fen, Suffolk, and at a Beaker settlement site at Belle Tout, Sussex, excavations have revealed very dense scatters of contemporary sherds of pottery in restricted areas near the occupation sites, but with no evidence of other activities. These areas have been interpreted as possible gardens, where the ground was intensively manured for special crops.

What crops were grown on these suggested prehistoric gardens? Here the archaeologist has to rely on the identification of pollen remains sealed on old ground surfaces or seed impressions accidentally baked into pieces of pottery. The results of this work are difficult to interpret for it seems that throughout most of the prehistoric period the variety of crops grown was very limited. Cereals of various types were almost ubiquitous, though flax is also recorded and beans seem to have appeared in later prehistoric times. Yet none of these can be considered as garden plants that would have necessitated special areas and treatment unless plots for raising seeds are envisaged. However, there are records in prehistoric contexts of a number of species of plants which are today regarded as weeds but which were certainly used as food by prehistoric man. Fat hen, whose seeds are rich in fat, black bindweed, Good King Henry, a spinach-like plant, and onion couch, a strongly tuberised plant, are all known from bronze age or iron age sites and may well have been grown as garden vegetables. On the whole, however, it remains difficult, using present archaeological techniques, to identify without doubt gardens of the prehistoric period.

For four hundred years after AD 43 most of Britain lay within the Roman Empire. It was during this period that the first pleasure gardens that can be identified appeared in Britain.

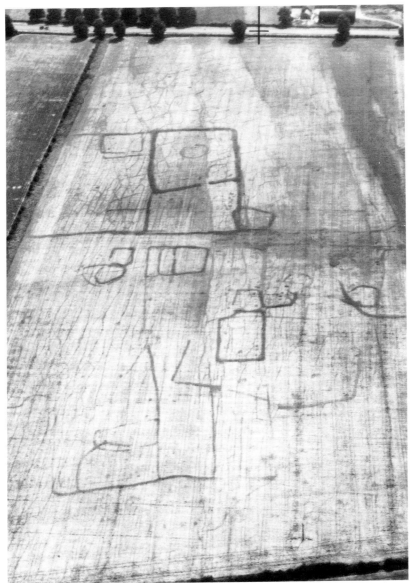

Plate 15. Iron age settlement, Thorpe Achurch, Northamptonshire. This hamlet lies on modern arable land and its outlines are only visible as crop marks. Circular hut sites and paddocks can be recognised but again the smaller enclosures could have been used as garden plots. (Copyright: Cambridge University Collection.)

Roman pleasure gardens were just one aspect of Roman civilisation which flowered precariously for a few centuries and then quickly disappeared. As we noted earlier, most Roman villas probably had gardens, yet few have been found as archaeologists have concentrated on the structures of villas, their foundations, mosaic pavements and bath suites rather than on the contemporary gardens.

The remains of pleasure gardens do exist and can be identified. Roman gardens were direct imports from the Mediterranean and had, with only minor modifications, the appearance of classical gardens. This means that they were physically attached to the villas and were generally enclosed either by walls or by parts of the villa so that they formed courtyards. Within these enclosed courts there were usually rectilinear arrangements of paths, lined with flower beds or low hedges and often with statuary or water features in the centre, at intersections or along the paths. Such details have rarely survived on the ground at the sites of Roman villas, though some low scarps at the villa at Sudeley, Gloucestershire, within the area of the main courtyard, are almost certainly the remains of garden terraces although they have been interpreted as internal walled subdivisions (fig. 1).

Excavations give us the best picture of Roman gardens in Britain. The best known of these were carried out at the site of the early Roman palace at Fishbourne in West Sussex, where a large part of the gardens has been revealed. The gardens belonged to a building unique in Roman Britain, a palace which was built around AD 75. We do not know who owned it but he was a man of immense wealth, of high position and with knowledge of or access to the best of Roman material culture. It has been suggested that the owner was perhaps Cogidubnus, a native king who, as as result of his co-operation with the Roman conquerors, was allowed to retain his throne as a 'client king' within the administrative system of Roman Britain. Whoever the owner was, both palace and gardens were on a lavish scale. The palace itself consisted of four sumptuously decorated ranges set around a rectangular garden. This was very formal and linked the main entrance hall of the palace on the east with the splendid audience chamber on the west. The garden was thus not merely for pleasure but was intended to impress on visitors the status of its owner.

This formal garden, some 75 by 100 metres (250 by 325 feet) in extent, had a broad colonnade or verandah around it. Across the centre was a wide path while narrower paths encircled the garden on all four sides. The paths were edged by narrow trenches with equally spaced recesses. The trenches were filled with a rich soil and were cut into the underlying clay and gravel. They were almost certainly for low clipped hedges, probably of box. On the east side of the garden against the colonnade one trench was associated with postholes, suggesting the existence of a plant that required a timber structure, while nearby a row of postholes and pits probably indicated another timber framework supporting flowering trees or shrubs. It seems that these latter features were designed to provide a backdrop to the garden when viewed from the west.

Other important features recorded were waterpipes which ran around the outer edge of the encircling pathway. These perhaps served fountains or raised basins set along the paths in the recesses, for parts of a number of marble basins were discovered on the site. Though this magnificent garden was clearly the main one, it did not stand alone. On the south side of the palace, small-scale excavations revealed traces of a terraced garden extending down the slope towards the sea shore. Though the full details were not recovered, this appears to have been a much more informal garden than the other, with a stream, pond, fountain and randomly arranged trees and shrubs.

Fishbourne is the only Roman pleasure garden known in any detail. Elsewhere there are tantalisingly vague records concerning other gardens. At Sudeley, in addition to the possible terraces noted above, excavations revealed a roughly paved path exactly bisecting the walled courtyard. At Frocester, also in Gloucestershire, a fragment of the former garden dating from the early fourth century, and which lay in front of the villa, has been excavated. A drive approached the main entrance to the villa and this was flanked by turf verges with rectangular flower beds set within them. Where the drive widened to form a turning area in front of the house, it was bordered on the east by an extremely narrow bed, perhaps for a hedge, which was probably deliberately placed so that it screened the stokehole which fed the central heating. In front of the villa on either side of the drive, a gravel path was discovered, again with the remains of flower beds in front of it. On the west of the drive there was probably an orchard while to the east there was a paved area. One other notable discovery at Frocester was the remains of box plants in charcoal. This suggests the existence of low box hedges. Box has also been found at the villa at Farmoor, Oxfordshire, and though no certain gardens were discovered it is possible that the small enclosures around the house, said to be for purely agricultural purposes, were garden divisions.

At Rockbourne, Hampshire, the large villa is now known to have had at least one square walled garden, which was divided by gravel paths with an ornamental pond at the intersection and with a raised platform in one corner. At the Roman villa of Gorhambury, Hertfordshire, excavations have revealed two lines of postholes joined by a shallow trench with a cobbled path between them. This has been interpreted as a covered walkway leading towards the main house, supporting climbing plants.

Excavations of the great villa at Brading on the Isle of Wight indicated that a courtyard there had a gravel path along two sides and also led to the discovery of the foundations of a semicircular structure variously interpreted as a seated alcove or as a water feature.

There is little firm evidence of the plants grown in Roman pleasure gardens. The existence of box has already been noted and the discovery of seeds of grapes, plums, apples and sweet cherries shows that fruit orchards and vineyards certainly existed. A pruning knife found at a villa near East Grinstead, West Sussex, is another form of archaeological evidence for orchards. The types of flowers in Roman gardens are less well known, but the rose, lily, poppy and pansy are generally said to have been introduced into Britain in this period.

Roman pleasure gardens seem to have been restricted to the major villas. Most of the people of Roman Britain probably had only vegetable gardens. The problems of identifying Roman vegetable gardens are the same as for the prehistoric period, though we do have evidence that cabbages, parsnips, turnips and carrots were grown. In the silt fenlands of eastern England are hundreds of Roman villages, hamlets and farmsteads which were established early in Roman times. They can be seen on air photographs and all are surrounded by tiny closes or paddocks, often described as 'fields'. They are much more likely to have been stockyards or possibly gardens, though we cannot tell the difference at the moment. In a very different situation, in North Wales, is the great mountain-top fort of Tre'r Ceiri. The fort was occupied in the Roman period and just outside it are irregular clusters of ovoid enclosures, bounded by low walls, which were formed by clearing scree from the interiors. Again, while some may be cattle pens, it is likely, but unproven, that others could have been garden plots.

4
Medieval gardens

From Saxon times onwards the written historical record becomes increasingly useful for the archaeology of gardens though, at least for much of the early medieval period, references to gardens are vague. Numerous medieval documents note the existence of gardens at religious houses, manor houses, palaces and castles, but relatively few give any descriptions of their arrangements. More useful are a few late medieval illuminated manuscripts which give, perhaps idealised, views of medieval gardens. The main characteristic of medieval gardens was their small size. For example a 1249 building account for the royal palace at Woodstock in Oxfordshire includes details of a garden whose extent was the same as some rooms that were pulled down to create it.

The features of medieval gardens that interest the archaeologist are the surrounding walls or banks, sometimes with sitting-out places recessed within them or at corners, raised flower beds with stone or wooden revetments, stone seats, ornamental ponds, fountains and paved or gravel paths. All large monastic houses appear to have had gardens of some form and the almost ubiquitous cloisters were often in practice an enclosed garden with flower beds and ponds. Though these are some of the features which archaeologists should find in gardens, there is very little good evidence on the ground. The best has come from excavations on monastic sites. Work at Glastonbury Abbey, Somerset, led to the discovery, within the twelfth-century cloisters, of a stone-kerbed path surrounding a small area of finely worked soil, presumably a flower bed. At Polsloe Priory, in Devon, excavation revealed a tiny space only 10 by 30 metres (33 by 98 feet) on the south side of the cloister and bounded by the kitchen, dorter and a wall. It was filled with well tilled soil and has been interpreted as a garden though it may have been only a vegetable plot. In addition the often extensive closes and paddocks which lay outside the main monastic buildings may have been cultivated as gardens, though they certainly had other uses as well. At Bardney, Lincolnshire (plate 16), there are indications, even on the ground, of ranges of buildings, perhaps used for agricultural purposes. The special way of life of the Carthusian order, whereby each member occupied a small cell

Plate 16. Bardney Abbey, Lincolnshire. The outline of the church and the associated buildings surround the enclosed cloister, in effect a small garden. Beyond, various banks and ditches delimit paddocks and enclosures, some of which were probably cultivated for food. (Copyright: Cambridge University Collection.)

attached to a walled garden, has led to the identification of these gardens at the few British Carthusian houses. For example, at both Hinton, in Avon, and Mount Grace, in North Yorkshire, rows of tiny gardens measuring only 20 by 12 metres (66 by 39 feet), and arranged with their cells around the cloisters, have been discovered. Yet again very few details of the internal arrangements of the gardens have come to light. At Hinton one had a paved walk along one side while at Mount Grace all had a covered way on one wall and one had a 'tank', perhaps a water feature, within it.

Other excavational evidence, albeit of a negative kind, has come from work on moated sites. These moats are usually assumed to be the sites of medieval manor houses and they range greatly in shape and size and often have complex moated or embanked outworks. Medieval documents suggest that on large moated sites there were often several small gardens scattered among the buildings there. Each appears to have had its own surrounding hedges or fences and small ornamental ponds were

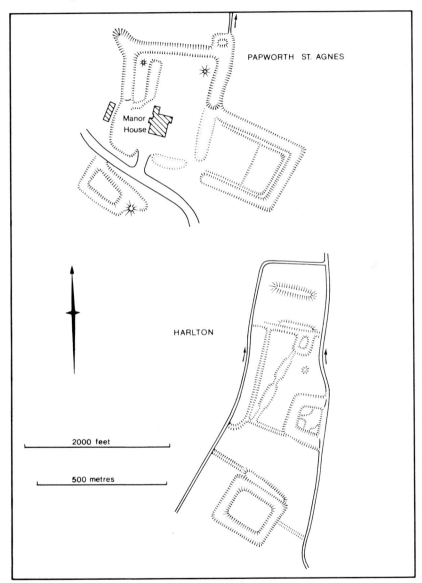

Fig. 8. Moated sites, Cambridgeshire. At Harlton the complex arrangement of moated enclosures, ponds and watercourses suggests that there may have been some gardens here in medieval times. The southern moat is the most likely position. At Papworth a rectangular medieval moat was remodelled and given outer ditched enclosures, all part of an elaborate garden, in 1585, when the manor house was rebuilt (see also plate 25). (After RCHM.)

not uncommon. Where the main moat covered only a small area and this was mostly occupied by buildings, the gardens apparently lay outside and were themselves often surrounded by water-filled ditches (plate 17; fig. 8).

Excavations on moated sites have consistently failed to find the remains of such gardens, or perhaps the features have been misinterpreted as fish-breeding tanks, farmyards and fowlhouses. Outer moated enclosures have also been examined and a common feature of these is that there is no occupation within them. A moat at Chalgrove, Oxfordshire, was excavated and, though the main moated island was found to have had continuous occupation from the twelfth century to the fifteenth, a small moated island attached to it had no structures or occupation whatsoever. Two other moats in Yorkshire, at Newsteads and at Rest Park, also had moated enclosures with no features within them. At another Yorkshire moat at East Haddlesey, documentary evidence indicated that one Miles Stapleton, the lord of the manor in the late thirteenth century, built a new house there surrounded by a moat and also constructed a garden within an outer moated enclosure. Again excavations on this presumed garden revealed no evidence of any activity. The lack of structures in these attached enclosures is not without interest. Archaeologists usually dig to find objects and structures. On most of the examples quoted the areas were quickly trenched to see if any possible structures existed and when nothing was found they were abandoned. The careful excavation techniques and support-ing scientific examinations were not carried out and thus the minor traces of gardens, such as those at the Roman site at Fishbourne, were probably missed.

The same is true of a number of excavations on isolated moated sites which have also been dug into, the excavations then being abandoned when nothing was found. Indeed there is now a large class of so called 'empty moats' which continue to puzzle archaeologists. While a number of these may have been constructed for a variety of reasons, some were probably the gardens of adjacent houses which have either long since disappeared or have been rebuilt. An example of this is at Epperstone, Nottinghamshire, where an empty moat lies at the bottom of a slope on which the post-medieval manor house stands. It is likely that this moat was a detached moated garden, the details of which were not recognised by the excavators.

Despite the lack of firm evidence from excavations, it is likely that moated gardens, of various forms, were a feature of upper

Plate 17. Moated site, Linwood, Lincolnshire. A typical medieval moated site. The main house probably stood on the large island to the left but the other island may have been a garden. (Copyright: Cambridge University Collection.)

middle class medieval life. This has an important bearing when we come to examine the evidence for early post-medieval gardens for there water-filled enclosures and still-water ponds were very common. It is possible that the tradition of a moated garden, established perhaps as early as the twelfth century, persisted long after moated sites themselves had become unfashionable.

If archaeologists have failed to find medieval pleasure gardens by excavation, a different picture emerges when we turn to examine the work carried out by field archaeologists. These are people who seek out the upstanding remains of the past whether they be bronze age fields, iron age forts or deserted medieval villages, make accurate surveys of them and attempt to interpret the results. Because of the work of these people, there is on record a small but growing number of almost complete abandoned medieval gardens. Perhaps the best of these is at Nettleham, in Lincolnshire. The site, which has been preserved in permanent pasture, is that of one of the palaces of the medieval bishops of Lincoln which was abandoned in the middle of the sixteenth century. Careful examination of the banks, scarps and ditches has led, not only to the recognition of a great courtyard with barns and paddocks, associated with the grass-grown foundations of the palace, but also to a small enclosed garden attached to one side of the palace itself. This gives us perhaps the most complete picture we have of a late medieval pleasure garden.

First, the garden is very small, only 60 metres (200 feet) long. It is enclosed on the north, west and south by a low rubble bank which must be the base of a former high stone wall, and on the east by the site of the palace. At the higher southern end is a broad flat terrace 13 metres (43 feet) wide which projects eastwards past the southern end of the palace. Below this main terrace is a narrower one from the centre of which runs a flat-topped bank only 100 millimetres (4 inches) high. This was clearly once a raised footpath between two rectangular flower beds, whose northern edges are marked by a tiny scarp. Below this scarp is a further rectangular area which has another raised footpath on the east separating it from a rectangular space to the north of the palace building. The whole site may be interpreted as an elaborate formal walled garden with terraces, paths and flower beds set into the sloping ground and with a separate compartment at the north-eastern end.

Another late medieval garden in Lincolnshire is that at the site of the priory of Premonstratensian canonesses at Orford. There a detailed survey has revealed the existence of what was probably a small garden. The higher end consists of an almost square area, only 20 metres (66 feet) across, bounded on three sides by a broad ditch. Most of the interior is occupied by a low, rectangular, flat-topped mound 15 by 8 metres (49 by 26 feet), with a walkway around it. On the fourth side the ground slopes down to a stream, which appears to have formed the boundary there. Running across this slope are some very low ridges, perhaps the remains of former flower beds. This garden must date to before 1539, when the priory was dissolved.

A third garden, also possibly of medieval date, has been found at Collyweston, Northamptonshire (fig. 9). The remains, though much damaged, consist of two sets of low terraces, bounded by scarps. One group has evidence of internal subdivisions, presumably flower beds. Below them, on the hillside, is a set of contemporary fishponds. Documentary evidence shows that the garden was partly remodelled soon after 1486, but that it perhaps originated somewhat earlier, in 1453-5. The 'stone borders', which one John Steynesmore was paid 6d for constructing, were perhaps the edging to the flower beds which still survive.

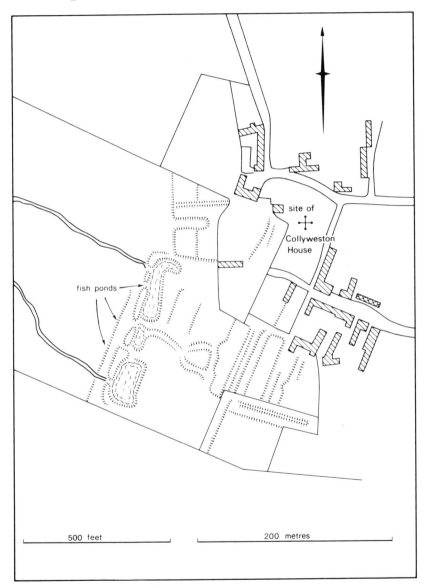

site of

Collyweston
House

fish ponds

500 feet

200 metres

Fig. 9. Collyweston, Northamptonshire. The first gardens were probably laid out here in 1453-4 but were remodelled in 1486, as were the fishponds to the west. Collyweston House was pulled down in the mid seventeenth century and the gardens abandoned. (After RCHM.)

There is little archaeological information on the plants grown in medieval pleasure or indeed vegetable gardens. The peony seeds recorded at Winchcombe Priory, Gloucestershire, are a rare example. This is perhaps no great loss to scholarship for, if the details of garden arrangements are lacking in medieval documents, those of plants are not and very full records of plants of all types exist for most of the late medieval period.

Former medieval vegetable gardens are much more common and may be recognised in almost every part of Britain. Many of the thousands of deserted medieval villages, as well as the numerous shrunken or moved village sites, are characterised by long narrow plots bounded by low banks, shallow ditches or scarps extending beyond the now empty house sites and yards (plate 18).

Once again excavation on such gardens has been almost non-existent for, despite the considerable number of excavated deserted villages, work has been concentrated almost entirely upon the houses and ancillary buildings. At Wharram Percy, in North Yorkshire, there is evidence that parts of the garden plots, from the thirteenth century onwards, were used as quarries to provide chalk necessary for building material, but otherwise there is no information about how these medieval garden plots functioned. Field examination sometimes indicates slight scarps subdividing the gardens, shallow ponds and other depressions. Well marked mounds, perhaps only of rubbish, are also common, as in the gardens of the deserted village of Croxby, in Lincolnshire. Other features include what appear to be the sites of small structures which may, on excavation, prove to be merely pigsties.

5
Gardens from the sixteenth to the early eighteenth century

From the mid sixteenth century onwards information on gardens increases rapidly. Plans, views, details of plants and treatises on garden management and design all become common. There is thus no problem in seeing what gardens were like and their owners and creators are often recorded. For the archaeologist too there is a very large quantity of material, usually in the form of upstanding well preserved earthworks, and this body of material is rapidly increasing as more and more sites are recognised. The combination of plentiful documentation and abundant archaeological evidence means that the potential for garden archaeology in the post-medieval period is considerable.

From the middle of the sixteenth century to the beginning of the eighteenth century gardens were mainly formal. Though there were many changes in detail, the recurring features of most pleasure gardens at this time were terraces, mounts and ponds or canals and thus the abandonment of such gardens has left earthworks, often of considerable size, for the archaeologist to examine.

Abandoned gardens of this period all reflect the complex interplay between social aspirations, artistic aims, changing fashions, wealth and status. Many new ideas of garden design, and indeed species of plant, were being introduced from abroad during these years and, depending on the owner or creator of the garden, these features were mixed to a greater or lesser extent with older traditions. On the whole the richer and the more important the owner, the larger and more sophisticated the garden. Men of lesser status tended to have smaller, less complex gardens and were often slower in following fashion. The archaeologist looking at formal gardens is able to see some of the relationships between all these matters.

One of the earliest post-medieval pleasure gardens to be identified is that at Canons Ashby in Northamptonshire. It was laid out in 1540 by Sir John Cope on one side of a new house constructed from the ruins of the former priory and was abandoned in 1551 when a replacement house was erected some distance away. This garden had many of the features of a medieval garden including an inner moated enclosure attached to

Plate 18. Deserted village of Holworth, Dorset. This village was finally abandoned in the fifteenth century. Its main street is still clearly visible with small yards, in which the houses stood, alongside it. Beyond, long narrow paddocks or crofts are the gardens of the medieval peasants. (Copyright: Cambridge University Collection.)

the house and a group of still-water ponds in an outer garden. Yet this latter feature was bounded, not by a confining wall, but by a flat-topped terrace walk, the perambulation of which allowed views across the adjacent countryside as well as of the internal garden. Thus it combined the traditional idea of a garden, with its enclosed spaces, with new concepts abandoning the old cloistered effect.

A later garden, on a grander scale as befitted its owner, is that outside the walls of Raglan Castle in Gwent. The castle was remodelled in the mid sixteenth century by the third Earl of Worcestershire and became a residence rather than a fortress, with its gardens laid out between 1570 and 1589. They were arranged in the bottom and along the sides of a valley, immediately below the castle wall, and thus the natural landscape provided the chance to create long earthen terraces and rectangular ponds. Many other details, including the footings of summerhouses on the ends of the terraces from where the garden could be viewed, still survive. The reason for this survival is that the castle was badly damaged in the siege of 1646 and the family therefore left it and moved to Badminton in Avon, where they erected a new house with its own gardens.

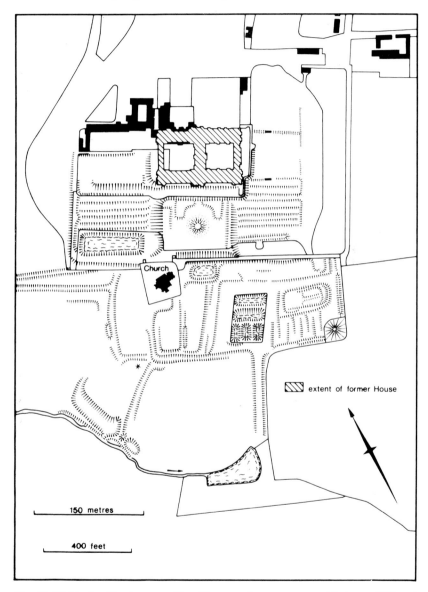

Fig. 10. Holdenby, Northamptonshire. These gardens were created between 1579 and 1587 by Sir Christopher Hatton. They are perhaps the best preserved of all sixteenth-century gardens in Britain and show magnificently what a great Elizabethan politician and landowner could achieve (see also plates 19 and 20). (After RCHM.)

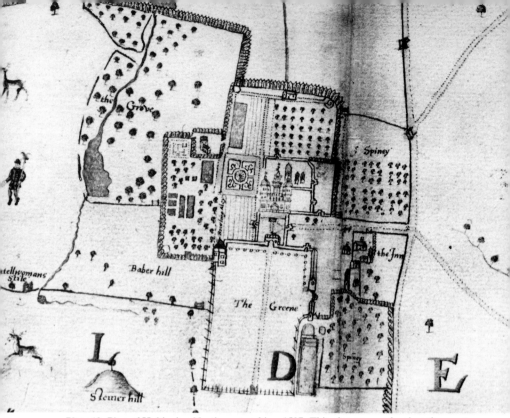

Plate 19. Plan of Holdenby, Northamptonshire, 1587. This plan was made when the great house at Holdenby had just been completed (see also fig. 10). (Northampton Record Office.)

Even more magnificent gardens are those at Holdenby in Northamptonshire, created, again to go with a new house, between 1579 and 1587 by Sir Christopher Hatton. Here, with the help of contemporary maps and descriptions, we can appreciate not only what a great pleasure garden looked like, but how it was created (plates 19, 20; fig. 10).

Hatton's new house was set uncompromisingly on the crest of a hill dominating the landscape. The gardens were intended to be laid out on the slopes of the hill and on the flat ground to the east. However, an obstacle to this was the existence of the village of Holdenby, which was in effect two villages, one with a parish church on the hillside, the other just north-east of the new house. Hatton swept both away, leaving only the church to be incorporated into the garden. The upper village was then recreated with a rectangular plan, laid out axially to the garden, which had views from the main courtyard through an arch on to the new square village green (plate 20). The construction of the gardens was carried out at the same time. On the south side of the house thousands of tons of earth were dumped on the hillside to create a level platform 80 by 100 metres (260 by 330 feet) projecting into the valley. On it elaborate flower beds, some of which still survive, were laid out. On either side of the platform two flights of seven terraces were dug and planted with rose bushes. At the bottom of one flight was a large rectangular pond, while a long narrow bowling green was laid out at the base of the other. On the hillside above, linking the new village to this formal garden, a large walled courtyard, with elaborately decorated archways, and a gatehouse were built. Beyond, a huge hedged area of lawns, bisected by an approach drive and with a two-storey banqueting hall and a lake, was created. On the lower slopes of the hillside to the south there was a carefully designed 'wilderness' of trees bounded by a wooden fence on a bank with a private flower garden in one corner, a group of rectangular ponds

Plate 20. Gateway, Holdenby, Northamptonshire. This gate, one of two, stood at the top of the eastern terraced garden and gave access to the entrance court. It also provided a vista, via its companion, to the newly planned village beyond (see also fig. 10). (Crown Copyright.)

in the centre and an elaborate arrangement of sloping terraced pathways leading up to a high 'mount' or circular mound. This superb garden lasted until 1651 when the house and all the other buildings were demolished. The area was later turned into a park and today almost all the details of this once magnificent arrangement survive in grassland.

An unusual type of garden remains which has recently come to light as a result of aerial photography is that at Elvetham, in Hampshire. In 1591 Edward Seymour, Earl of Hertford, entertained Elizabeth I there. To meet the demands of the occasion, which required accommodation and entertainment for the Queen and several hundred guests, the Earl not only enlarged his house but created a special garden for a water pageant. A crescent-shaped lake was constructed in which three islands, one arranged as a ship, another as a fort and the third as a spiral mount, were raised. The whole arrangement was an ephemeral feature, intended for one day's entertainment and then abandoned. Further, the house itself has long since disappeared and the area of the lake is now modern arable. Even so aerial photography has revealed the outlines of this lake and thus greatly added to the details preserved in documents and in an early nineteenth-century copy of a lost sixteenth-century original plan.

The unfinished gardens at Lyveden New Bield, Northamptonshire, begun by Sir Thomas Tresham in 1597, are also of great interest from the archaeological point of view (fig. 7). Not only do the canals, terraces with triple level paths, great circular mounds with spiral walkways and mounds of double truncated pyramidal form all still survive under the protection of modern copses, but other forms of archaeological investigation have added greatly to the picture. For though part of the gardens has been destroyed by modern cultivation, air photographs taken before this occurred show clearly that when the construction work came to an end, some of the half-completed terraces lay on top of medieval plough ridges. More interestingly, the modern destruction, when combined with later air photography, revealed new and unknown details. In the centre of the intended garden air photographs showed two blocks of parallel rows of pits, separated by an axial pathway, all visible as crop marks. These pits are the holes for the trees of the great 'wilderness' or orchard, which was meant to divide the garden into two parts. Elsewhere on the same site, careful field walking on newly ploughed fields led to the discovery of an intersecting pattern of strips of gravel set in the natural clay. These are paths of an elaborate knot

Plate 21. Kirby Hall, Northamptonshire. These magnificent gardens are arranged exactly as they were laid out in the 1680s as the edging to the paths and flower beds was discovered still in its original position. However, what is visible is less than one third of the seventeenth-century garden, which once extended to the right, across the stream and up the adjacent hillside. (Copyright: Cambridge University Collection.)

garden, which was completely unsuspected before work began. These gravel paths have survived because of the way they were built. Sir Thomas, no doubt well aware of the heavy nature of the soil at Lyveden, wrote to his clerk of works in 1597 and instructed him to form such paths by digging trenches up to 1 metre (3 feet) deep and to fill them with gravel. This was to ensure that ladies walking in the garden would keep their feet dry!

A much smaller garden, but one where archaeology was important in its understanding, is at Leighton Bromswold in Cambridgeshire. Today it is a rectangular area of ground bounded on three sides by a low flat-topped terrace or walkway with prospect mounds set on the corners. It was recognised as a garden as early as 1926 and at the same time its date, 1616, and its builder, Sir Gervaise Clifton, were noted. Yet it was stated then, and again by later scholars, that the accompanying house was never built. More careful examination in recent years has shown that the house was indeed built for the slight traces of its foundation walls still exist and match almost exactly the architect's plan which has also survived. Traces of the original flower beds and formal ponds were also discovered. An added complication, not unknown with such garden remains, was that the whole site was superimposed on a holloway lined by former paddocks and closes. These were the remains of the main street, houses and gardens of part of Leighton village which had been deserted centuries before the garden was built.

A later garden, notable for a number of factors related to archaeology, is that at Kirby Hall, Northamptonshire (plate 21). The great house was built in the late sixteenth century and then had its own small garden. In 1680 Sir Christopher Hatton IV destroyed the parish church and the small village of Kirby, then lying just outside the walls of the house, and laid out a magnificent garden nearly 570 metres (620 yards) long and 100 metres (110 yards) wide and divided into walled compartments which stretched across the adjoining valley. On Sir Christopher's death in 1706 the house and gardens were neglected. It was not until the twentieth century that the house was taken into guardianship by the Department of the Environment, and clearance of the garden revealed not only the brick and stone revetments of the terraces but also the limestone kerbs of the flower beds of the northern third of the garden. This part of the original garden has now been restored, making it a very rare example of a true seventeenth-century garden. More recent field walking of the land once occupied by the other two-thirds of the garden has led to the discovery of more kerb stones and traces of the boundary walls, which have confirmed the rather coarse details of the original garden, shown on a map of 1720.

By the late seventeenth century the arrangement of gardens was changing under the influence of new ideas from abroad and especially from France. One of the greatest of these French gardens is at Boughton, Northamptonshire (plates 7, 8). The gardens there were laid out on the orders of Ralph Montagu, later first Duke of Montagu, between 1685 and 1709. Montagu had been the British ambassador in Paris during the 1660s and 1670s and was much influenced by French ideas. The new garden was planned to go with Montagu's addition, entirely in the late seventeenth-century French style, to the old house at Boughton. To make the garden, the river Ise was diverted into a series of long straight 'canals', and other canals, rectangular ponds and an extensive arrangement of terraced flower beds, walkways and contrived wooded areas were constructed. This great garden was

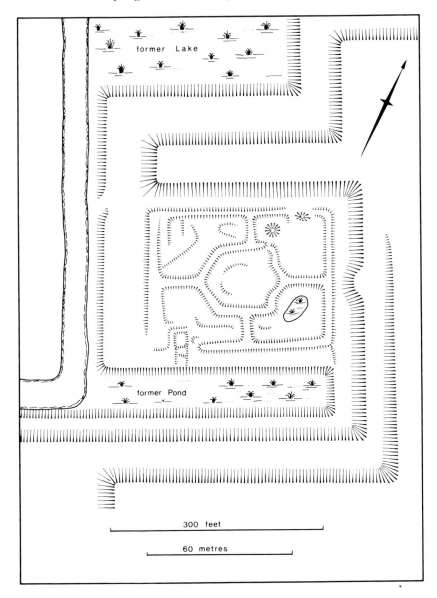

former Lake

former Pond

300 feet

60 metres

Fig. 11. Boughton, Northamptonshire. Within the remains of the enclosing terraced walks and formal ponds, the minute traces of the early eighteenth-century flower beds, less than 100 millimetres (4 inches) high, have been recognised and planned. (After RCHM.)

subsequently altered in detail at least twice, but in 1750 the last Duke died and the estate passed, through the female line, to the Buccleuch family. This resulted in the abandonment of the house as a permanent home and coincided with a major change in garden fashion. Most of the gardens were grassed over and incorporated into the landscaped park. As a consequence most of the constructed features were fossilised in the new grassland.

The recovery by archaeologists of the details of this garden, however, involved more than merely detailed surveys of these extant remains. The surveys were important and among other things led to the discovery of some of the original 1680 flower beds (fig. 11), ponds and the channels of the elaborate water gardens, as well as the more obvious terraces and canals. Other techniques were used, including the study of air photographs taken about 1950, which revealed evidence of other flower beds which had been destroyed by modern cultivation. More importantly perhaps, the results of modern estate improvement not only produced exciting information but indicated the potential for controlled archaeological excavation on such gardens.

In the south-west corner of the gardens at Boughton Ralph Montagu constructed an elaborate water feature known as the Star Pond. This was much admired by his contemporaries, a number of whom described it. It consisted of a sunken rectangular area of water with circular projections on three sides. It was surrounded by walkways and apparently fed by water from one of the high-level canals pouring over a series of steps known as the Cascade. On either side of the Cascade was a row of fountains which threw water upwards and at an angle so that it fell back on to the Cascade itself. In addition there were other fountains within the pond, one in each corner of each projection and a group in the centre. All these fountains were removed and the Cascade was replaced by a simple waterfall in the 1720s, while later neglect and alterations reduced the pond to an irregular depression fed by leakage from the canal.

In 1975 the pond was partially drained and dredged as part of modern estate management. This work was observed by archaeologists and many new features were revealed. The lower part of the Cascade steps was found to survive below the modern water level as did a low-level walkway, set at the original water's edge, paved with stones and bounded by elm-wood kerbs which projected into the pond at intervals. The edge of the depression in which the pond lay was seen to have been revetted in stone with pilaster buttresses and surmounted by a stone balustrade.

The revetment still existed as did the scars of the buttresses, and a number of pieces of the balustrade were also recovered. Even complete earthenware spigots from the fountainhead were found. Other discoveries included wooden drainpipes, actually hollowed-out elm trunks, which showed that water from the adjacent water garden was passed underground into the Star Pond. The gardens at Boughton are not only a remarkable survival but show what can be achieved by the archaeological examination of such remains.

As already noted, the gardens at Boughton were remodelled on at least two occasions during their short life. For example, the original centrepiece of the garden was an octagonal pond. This was replaced by a rectangular one in 1721 and then doubled in size in 1725. On the latter occasion also a raised square 'mount' was created and most of the earlier flower beds were grassed over. Yet the archaeological survey was able to notice these changes and in particular to recognise the complex layout of the original flower beds. Radical changes in arrangement, which were characteristic of all gardens as fashions changed, are important features which garden archaeologists must be prepared for. This is well demonstrated by a garden at Stainfield, in Lincolnshire, which lacks the detailed documentation of Boughton. The elaborate seventeenth-century terraced garden with its enclosed wilderness beyond, lying on top of the older deserted village of Stainfield, was partly remodelled and partly abandoned in the late seventeenth or early eighteenth century when a new layout with a tree-lined vista, edged by low banks, was constructed on a new axis. Yet both phases are clearly visible when the remains are accurately recorded. This kind of work is important when, as at Stainfield, documents giving details of such changes do not exist.

Even where documents, and especially contemporary plans, are available, archaeological work can sometimes show that they are wrong. A contemporary plan of Sir George Downing's early eighteenth-century garden at Gamlingay, Cambridgeshire, shows that its eastern edge was lined by a series of small rectangular ponds arranged in two lines at right angles to each other. As these ponds still survive (plate 4; fig. 4) it is possible to see that, because of the natural formation of the land, they could not be, nor were, laid out in the way the plan indicates but were set in a much less formal manner. Similarly an early eighteenth-century plan of a small seventeenth-century garden at Barnwell, Northamptonshire, shows its gravel paths, 'garden knotts', a terrace

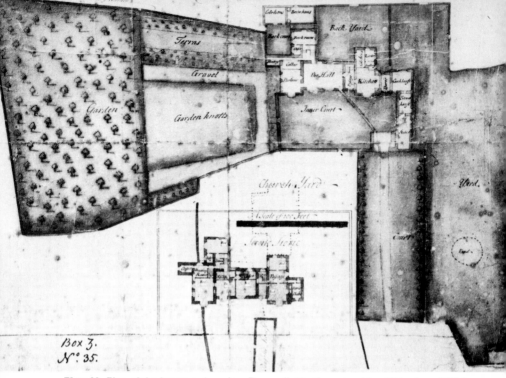

Plate 22. Plan of the house and garden, Barnwell, Northamptonshire. This plan of 1716 depicts a small manor house and its simple garden, perhaps of early seventeenth-century date. The plan fails to show that the division between the area of trees (the wilderness) and 'garden knotts' and the 'terras' was actually a raised terrace or walkway with a summerhouse at one end (see also fig. 12). (By permission of His Grace the Duke of Buccleuch.)

and a wilderness (plate 22). Yet not only do all these still survive on the ground, but a completely unrecorded high-level terrace or walkway separating the main garden from the wilderness, with the foundations of a summerhouse at one end, exists (plate 23; fig. 12).

On the other hand contemporary plans may show the site of a garden that otherwise could not be recognised even though the remains of it exist. The manor house, lying next to the church, at the village of Hardwick, Northamptonshire, is surrounded by earthworks (plate 24). These include old quarries, medieval plough ridges, a line of fishponds and a series of ditched enclosures. The fishponds and the enclosures are probably all medieval in date and were once part of the medieval manor farm. One of the enclosures extends from the manor house garden into the adjacent field. On the ground or from the air it appears identical to its neighbours. Yet a map of 1587 shows this enclosure with an elaborate set of intersecting flower beds within

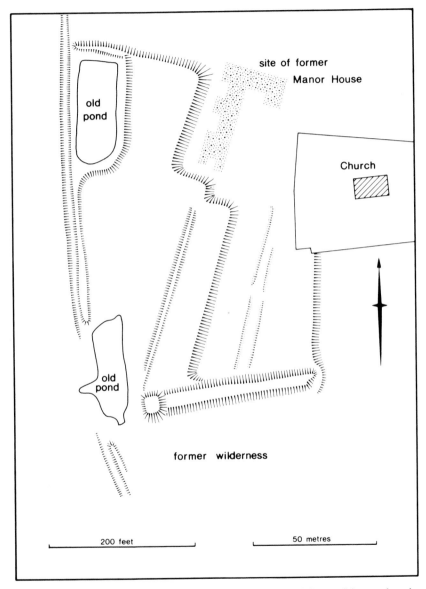

Fig. 12. Barnwell, Northamptonshire. This accurate survey of the surviving earthworks complements the evidence depicted on an early plan of these seventeenth-century gardens and suggests that the gardens were more sophisticated than the plan indicates (see also plates 22 and 23). (After RCHM.)

it. As the manor house was rebuilt in 1567-8 the garden is probably contemporary. The house survived but the garden was abandoned by 1684, probably because the house had declined in status and become a working farm.

Sometimes archaeological techniques can be used to solve problems connected with the development of gardens. At Blenheim Palace, Woodstock, Oxfordshire, early eighteenth-century plans show an arrangement of rectangular ponds close to the great bridge, in an area now covered by the later lake. Some scholars doubted whether these ponds ever existed and suggested that the plans were proposals that were never executed. However, air photographs taken in a very dry summer, when the lake was relatively shallow, showed the outlines of the ponds, just below the surface.

The continental influences on gardens at the end of the seventeenth century led to the establishment of parks beyond the formal gardens themselves. At Boughton the gardens discussed above were only part of a much larger area of emparking laid out at the same time. The formal gardens became more open with long views across them which were then carried out on to adjoining parkland to create vistas. The introduction of the ha-ha

Plate 23. Garden remains, Barnwell, Northamptonshire. This shows the terrace or walkway between the wilderness which lay to the right and the 'garden knotts' on the left. The foreground was the 'terras' shown on the 1716 plan (see also fig. 12). (Crown Copyright.)

Plate 24. Manorial site and garden, Hardwick, Northamptonshire. The sixteenth-century manor house lies just left of centre and above the church. Beyond in the valley are medieval fishponds and to the left of centre are various paddocks of medieval date, cut into by later quarries. The slight ditched enclosure to the right of the manor house with a line of trees cutting its upper right-hand corner is the site of the formal gardens shown on a plan of 1587. (Copyright: Cambridge University Collection.)

or sunken fence by the landscape architect Bridgeman helped this development. The outlying parks, however, were not the naturalised areas of the later eighteenth century. Nature still had to be tamed and ordered. As a result avenues were arranged in radiating lines, copses and woods were regimented into rectangles and squares, while features to help carry the eye from formal garden to formal park were introduced.

The gardens at Eastbury, Dorset, designed by Bridgeman in the early eighteenth century, are a splendid example of this, as well as being of interest in terms of archaeological discovery (fig. 3). They were found by archaeologists scanning air photographs for bronze age barrows. In a modern arable field, adjacent to the remains of Eastbury House, two parallel lines of low mounds were noted. These were obviously not bronze age barrows, but they were visited on the ground to see what they were. The formal gardens of Eastbury were then discovered, buried in the adjoining woodland. In addition to flower beds, terraces, ponds and ha-has, two huge mounds, of octagonal form, with battered faceted sides and with rounded summits, were found. The small mounds out in the parkland were then understood. They were to carry the eye of the viewer from the garden, past the great mounds, over the ha-ha and into the park. Further work revealed that the irregular copses of the late eighteenth-century parkland contained fragments of the rectangular enclosure banks set around the early eighteenth-century plantations.

All the examples of gardens discussed so far are relatively large and complex and belonged to the members of the highest classes of sixteenth and seventeenth-century society. Far more common, and perhaps even more important to discover and record, are the gardens of lesser people. These are usually quite unknown and few documents survive to explain them. At the tiny and remote village of Hamerton, Cambridgeshire, examination of what had previously been described as a medieval moated site proved that it was a small but magnificent late sixteenth or early seventeenth-century garden with terraces, cut into the sloping ground, with a long canal and a terraceway beyond, and a large 'mount' and moated water garden attached. Despite the most assiduous searching of contemporary documents, only one reference to its existence, in 1625, has been found. Even more curious was the discovery of a late seventeenth- or early eighteenth-century garden near the village of Haddenham out on a fen island in Cambridgeshire. Again, a canal, flower beds and a large trapezoidal pond, fed by a cascade, were all discovered preserved in grassland. Yet not a single document which mentions it has been located.

There are also many very small gardens which were newly built in the sixteenth or seventeenth century or which were attached to earlier medieval moated sites. These are probably very common but require careful examination of the remains to decide their real purpose. A number have been discovered in west Cambridgeshire and two examples will show the problems as well as the results. One is a moated site known as Croydon Wilds, set in a remote corner of Croydon parish. It seems to be a typical moated site, in an area of former woodland, and thus to be the remains of a twelfth- to fourteenth-century secondary settlement. However, after a detailed survey, the moat was seen to be exactly square, with terraced walkways along two sides of the interior and with mounds in each corner. Records of an early seventeenth-century

Plate 25. Papworth St Agnes Manor House, Cambridgeshire. This small but distinguished house was built in 1585 on the site of an older manor house which stood within a rectangular moated site. The moat was remodelled to become a garden for the house and the bay window overlooked one of the new garden compartments, which extended south-west beyond the original moat (see also fig. 8). (Crown Copyright.)

house, now demolished, known to have stood in the centre of the moat, proved conclusively that the site was a garden, though again no record of it existed in documents.

A different type of site is that at Papworth St Agnes, Cambridgeshire (plate 25; fig. 8). The medieval manor house acquired, probably in the thirteenth or fourteenth century, a rectangular moat around it. In 1585 the manor house was rebuilt and the moat transformed into a formal garden. A pond was dug within the interior of the moated site and two prospect mounds were constructed at the corners. In addition a section of the moat to the south was filled in and replaced by a long enclosure, bounded by a low bank and shallow ditch, which projected outwards into the adjacent field. This was for a formal flower garden to be viewed from the great bay window of the new house. Other features include a separate moated garden to the south-

Plate 26. The King's Knot, Stirling Castle, Scotland. Though partly restored in 1867, these earthworks are the remains of a garden laid out in 1627-8 to the south-west of the castle. (Copyright: Cambridge University Collection.)

east. In both these instances we see the older tradition of a moat, transformed in different ways into a later garden.

Most of the foregoing examples are from England. But the sites of former gardens are not confined to that country. Scotland, in particular, has many examples, although there other traditions and fashions have produced different remains. A garden, not dissimilar to English ones, still remains below the castle at Stirling, dating from 1627-8 (plate 26). There is an elaborate central mound, surrounded by terraces and with traces of other terraces and formerly walled compartments on either side. However, the site was extensively restored in 1867 and may not be close to the original form. More characteristic of Scotland are the so-called 'hanging gardens' or flights of terraces which often occupied the steep slopes around sixteenth- and seventeenth-century Scottish country houses. Neidpath Castle, near Peebles, has such a flight on the valley side above the river Tweed. Not far away, the late sixteenth-century tower house of Elibank Castle, near Galashiels, has terraces on all four sides of the small plateau on which it stands. As in England the survival of such remains is usually the result of the abandonment of the house or a decline in its status. At Elibank the house and gardens were constructed soon after 1595. In 1621 its builder was in social disgrace and died a few months later. By 1722 the castle was already in ruins and the garden derelict.

6
Parks and gardens of the eighteenth and nineteenth centuries

From the middle of the eighteenth century the concept of gardens changed. Formal arrangements, set around houses with geometrically laid-out parks beyond, rapidly went out of fashion and were replaced by 'naturalised' parkland which swept to the walls of the houses. This was the era of Capability Brown, though he is only the best known of a number of landscape designers who created tens of thousands of acres of new landscapes in the late eighteenth and early nineteenth centuries. Although these parks look, and were intended to look, 'natural', this was often the result of prodigious feats of engineering, requiring the removal of large quantities of earth on a scale far beyond that of even the most complex terraces of earlier gardens.

The majority of such parks still survive, but they too have been altered and rearranged in succeeding years. The task of the archaeologist can be said to be twofold. It is to identify the major construction features connected with the naturalisation of the landscape and to discover and interpret aspects of these parks which have been left as relict features as a result of later changes.

The identification of constructional remains is often difficult for the intention was to disguise such work and to give an entirely natural appearance. Nevertheless such remains can be identified if the landscape is examined with care. For example, at Fawsley, in Northamptonshire, the park created by Capability Brown has as its centrepiece a great lake, or so it appears when viewed from the house. The lake begins close to the hall itself and seems to stretch the full length of the park, entirely filling a broad open valley. In fact it is not one pond, but two. A single lake would have been impossible to construct for it would have required a huge dam and would have covered half the park. Brown cunningly set one pond slightly below the first, so that, viewed from upstream, the dam is almost invisible and the land seems to be dominated by a single sheet of water. Careful observation of this type not only allows us an understanding of the mechanics of the construction but also enables us better to appreciate the achievement of a designer such as Brown.

A variation on this kind of work can be seen at Althorp, also in Northamptonshire. Here the old house, though enlarged and

Plate 27. Triumphal arch and earthworks, Horton, Northamptonshire. The arch today stands clear of the backdrop of trees and is visible from a distance. However, the small ditched enclosures containing numerous tree holes on either side of it indicate that when it was built in the mid eighteenth century it was intended to be partly obscured by trees. (Crown Copyright.)

altered, remains on its sixteenth-century site. The formal gardens which lay around it were removed in the 1730s and a new landscape park appeared. One important feature of the park was to be an avenue of trees extending along the rising ground from the centre of the house. Yet merely to plant the trees would not have created the desired effect, for some 400 metres (¼ mile) from the house a natural spur sloped down across its line, partially obscuring the intended view. The problem was solved by the Spencers, or their unknown gardener, by cutting away the end of the spur entirely. The result is that the spur now ends with an abrupt scarp 2.5 metres (8 feet) high and almost 200 metres (220 yards) long. The rest has disappeared and the avenue now extends across continuously rising ground.

In addition, also at this avenue at Althorp, we can see an example of the second type of feature which field archaeologists should look for. The park is of necessity on land which was under

Plate 28. Watford Court, Watford, Northamptonshire. This photograph illustrates graphically the complexities of past activities fossilised in landscaped parks. In the foreground are the remains of house sites, gardens and plough ridges of part of the medieval village of Watford. In the background are other garden plots. All these were incorporated into the park when it was laid out in the early eighteenth century. At that time the park had a rigidly formal appearance with a sunken tree-lined drive across it, now the holloway, and with a group of rectangular ponds. In the mid nineteenth century the park was made less formal. (Copyright: Cambridge University Collection.)

cultivation in the medieval period and large areas of it are covered by remains of ridge-and-furrow ploughing. But along the line of the avenue, and indeed along other avenues in the park, the ridge-and-furrow has been carefully flattened and replaced by a raised carriage drive or path, 6 metres (20 feet) wide and only 0.25 metres (10 inches) high. This shows that the avenue was intended to be used as an access way as well as a view.

At Horton, also in Northamptonshire, there are other remains worth noting. There, the formal gardens were swept away in the 1740s by the second Earl of Halifax less than twenty years after they had been enlarged by his father. The Earl laid out an informal landscaped park, along the edges of which lay a number of architectural features including a triumphal arch, a classical temple and a building used as a menagerie. All this survives today and appears to be exactly as intended. Yet ground examination has shown that, for example, in front of the triumphal arch and the menagerie are curving ditches and banks, enclosing a number of holes where trees formerly stood (plate 27). Elsewhere are circular ditches also enclosing tree holes. It thus seems that the park was intended to look different from its present appearance. The triumphal arch was apparently not meant to be seen standing before a backdrop of trees, but almost surrounded by trees and only just visible.

Not all the earthwork remains in eighteenth- and nineteenth-century parkland need be connected with gardens or emparking: indeed the majority are not. Emparking fossilised under grass much more than former gardens and such parks are one of the most important preservation agents for archaeological sites of all periods. Most lowland parks preserve large areas of medieval ridge-and-furrow but often include the remains of former farmsteads, medieval moats, watermills and a host of other types of site (plate 28). Very common are the remains of deserted villages, some of which were abandoned in the fourteenth, fifteenth and sixteenth centuries, but many of which were destroyed to make way for the parks themselves (plate 29). Those villages cleared away in recent times are useful in that their remains sometimes incorporate former vegetable gardens of the lower orders of society at this period.

One of the best examples of this is at Milton Abbas in Dorset (fig. 13). There, until the late eighteenth century, a small town existed in the valley bottom, next to the great medieval abbey church and the house erected out of the former monastic buildings. Then in 1770 Joseph Damer, later Viscount Milton, rebuilt the house and started to remove the town. By 1790 the town had gone, its inhabitants rehoused in a new estate village, and a great park was laid out around the house. The earthwork fragments of the main street and former house sites still exist, but best of all are the abandoned gardens of a group of houses which lay along Back Street. There are fourteen rectangular closes bounded by low banks, extending up the valley side, each once the vegetable garden behind a house. They show exactly the arrangements of humble gardens of this type at the end of the eighteenth century. Six of them have the foundations of small structures at their far ends, which may be pigsties or possibly outside privies. One has no features within it, but all the rest have low terraces of various forms, presumably marking divisions

Plate 29. Boughton Park, Northamptonshire. In the background is Boughton House, on the site of the medieval manor house of Boughton, but massively rebuilt in the late seventeenth century. In the foreground, the uneven nature of the land marks the site of the village of Boughton, deserted in the fifteenth century but preserved by the existence of the park created in the early eighteenth century. (Crown Copyright.)

between individual vegetable plots.

The laying out of parks around new and rebuilt country houses continued right through the nineteenth century, but it gradually became fashionable to construct more traditional gardens around the houses themselves. These were sometimes quite formal but in other cases were very informal. The results are the gardens that now surround many country houses. These are often Victorian in appearance, with balustraded terraces and flower beds. Such gardens do not offer as much to the archaeologist as those of earlier periods. Most are still in existence and there is usually a wealth of documentation and even photographs to show how they were built and what they looked like. Even so they should not be totally ignored. The pressures of the post-war years have resulted in the desertion and demolition of dozens of great nineteenth-

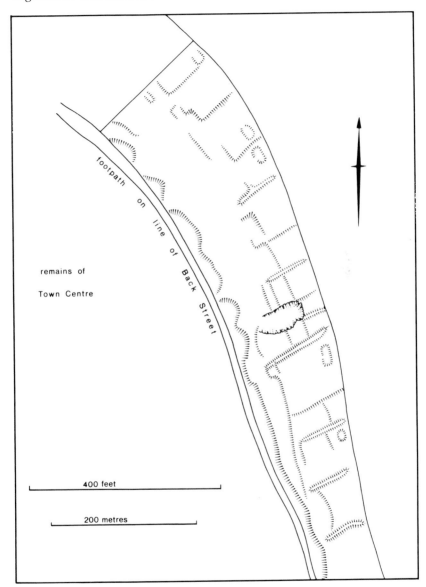

Fig. 13. Milton Abbas, Dorset. These house sites and gardens were part of the small market town of Milton Abbas. The whole town was removed in the late eighteenth century and replaced by a landscaped park. (After RCHM.)

century country houses and their gardens have thus returned to
the wild as their predecessors of the sixteenth and seventeenth
centuries did. Overgrown Victorian gardens are becoming very
common. The archaeologist can work on these as well as those of
earlier times, often with the further advantage that the minor
features, lost in the older gardens, are still visible. For example,
at Stanford, Norfolk, the nineteenth-century gardens of Buck-
enham Tofts Hall were finally left when the army took over the
area for training in 1940. The flower beds, terraces, paths and
even the wrought iron trellises for roses still survive today.

   Some Victorian gardens survive as earthworks even when the
house is still occupied. Because of the expense of keeping up
elaborate gardens, with their flower beds, many have been
grassed over in recent years. One such is at Muncaster Castle, in
Cumbria, where a fine nineteenth-century garden comprising
sunken areas and raised terraces is still visible in the broad lawns
which now occupy the area in front of the house.

7
Conclusion

It is hoped that by now the value of the archaeology of gardens is clear. The potential for new and exciting discoveries and for the deeper understanding of man's attempt to surround his home with beauty is considerable. Unlike most aspects of archaeology little work has been done, much can be achieved by both amateurs and professionals, and the rewards are immense. The greatest difficulty to the successful development of garden archaeology is in the mind of the archaeologist. He has to recognise the value of the study and, more important, to realise that abandoned gardens are there to be investigated. If this could be achieved then the example of the treatment of the seventeenth-century abandoned garden in a south Cambridgeshire village will not occur again. The remains of that garden are now almost destroyed, not by later gardeners, by nineteenth-century emparking nor indeed by modern farmers. They have been reduced to virtual obliteration by generations of archaeologists trying to prove, unsuccessfully, that they were a Roman camp, an iron age farm or a deserted medieval village.

8
Select bibliography

Garden history

Amherst, A. *A History of Gardens in England*. Bernard Quarditch, London, 1895.

Clark, H. F. *The English Landscape Garden*. 1948.

Dutton, R. *The English Garden*. Batsford, 1950.

Hadfield, M. *A History of British Gardens*. Hamlyn, 1969.

Harvey, J. *Medieval Gardens*. Batsford, 1981.

Hunt, J. D. and Willis, P. *The Genius of Place*. Paul Elek, 1975.

Hussey, C. *English Gardens and Landscapes 1700-1750*. Country Life, 1967.

Hyams, E. *A History of Gardens and Gardening*. 1971.

McLean, T. *Medieval English Gardens*. Collins, 1981.

Strong, R. *The Renaissance Garden in England*. Thames and Hudson, 1979.

Stroud, D. *Humphry Repton*. Country Life, 1962.

Stroud, D. *Capability Brown*. Faber and Faber, 1975.

Thacker, C. *The History of Gardens*. 1979.

Willis, P. *Charles Bridgeman and the English Landscape Garden*. Zwemmer, 1978.

Garden archaeology

Aston, M. 'Gardens and Earthworks at Hardington and Low Ham, Somerset'. *Proceedings Somerset Archaeological Society* 122 (1978), 11-28.

Aston, M. 'Salford, Oxfordshire'. Council for British Archaeology, Group 9 *Newsletter* 4 (1974), 16-18.

Aston, M. 'Earthworks at the Bishop's Palace, Alvechurch, Worcestershire.' *Transactions Worcestershire Archaeological Society* 3 (1970-2), 55-9.

Aston, M. and Rowley, T. *Landscape Archaeology*. 1974.

Brown, A. E. and Taylor, C. C. 'The Gardens at Lyveden, Northamptonshire'. *Archaeological Journal* 129 (1972), 154-60.

Brown, A. E. and Taylor, C. C. 'Cambridgeshire Earthwork Surveys II'. *Proceedings Cambridgeshire Antiquarian Society* 67 (1977), 85-94, 99-101.

Brown, A. E. and Taylor, C. C. 'Cambridgeshire Earthwork Surveys III'. *Proceedings Cambridgeshire Antiquarian Society* 68 (1978), 65-7.

Cunliffe, B. *Excavations at Fishbourne,* I (1971), 120-34.
Cunliffe, B. *Fishbourne: A Roman Palace and its Garden.* 1971.
Everson, P. 'Stallingborough - Earthworks Survey'. *Lincolnshire History and Archaeology* 16 (1981), 29-37.
Everson, P. 'Earthwork Survey in Lindsey'. *Moated Sites Research Group Report* 9 (1982), 13.
Le Patourel, H. E. J. 'The Excavation of Moated Sites' in F. A. Aberg (editor), *Medieval Moated Sites.* Council for British Archaeology Research Report 17 (1978), 40-1.
Mercer, R. (editor). *Farming Practice in British Prehistory.* 1981.
Steane, J. M. 'The Development of Tudor and Stuart Garden Design in Northamptonshire'. *Northamptonshire Past and Present* 5 (1977), 383-406.
Thompson, M. W. 'Reclamation of Waste Ground for the Pleasance at Kenilworth Castle, Warwickshire'. *Medieval Archaeology* 8 (1964), 222-3.
Thompson, M. W. 'Two Levels of the Mere at Kenilworth Castle, Warwickshire'. *Medieval Archaeology* 9 (1965), 156-61.
Wilson D. R. and Wilson, J. 'The Site of the Elvetham Entertainment'. *Antiquity* 56, number 216 (1982), 46-7.

The recent Inventories of the Royal Commissions on Historical Monuments for England and Scotland contain many plans and descriptions of garden remains. Particularly useful are:

RCHM (Eng.), *Dorset* II part 2 (1970): Wool (43).
RCHM (Eng.), *Dorset* III (1970): Milton Abbas (20).
RCHM (Eng.), *Dorset* IV (1972): Tarrant Gunville (2).
RCHM (Eng.), *Dorset* V (1975): Pentridge (2).
RCHM (Eng.), *West Cambridgeshire* (1968): lxi-lxvi for further references.
RCHM (Eng.), *North East Cambridgeshire* (1972): Bottisham (61), Fen Ditton (2) and Horningsea (33).
RCHM (Eng.), *The Town of Stamford* (1977): (96), (97), (276).
RCHM (Eng.), *Peterborough New Town* (1969): Longthorpe (7).
RCHM (Eng.), *Northamptonshire* I-IV (1975-82): contains over forty examples of abandoned gardens; see Indexes.
RCHM (Scot.), *Selkirk* (1957): (13), (16).
RCHM (Scot.), *Stirlingshire* I (1963): (219).
RCHM (Scot.) *Peeblesshire* (1967): (403), (515), (519), (525), (527).

Older Commission volumes also noted former gardens though these were not always recognised as such at the time. For

examples see:
RCHM (Eng.), *Essex* II (1921): Havering atte Bower (33), Stanstead Abbots (8).
RCHM (Eng.), *Herefordshire* III (1934): Aymestrey (34).
RCHM (Eng.), *Westmorland* (1936): Rydal and Laughrigg (36).

Index
Page numbers in italic refer to illustrations